PLANETARY:

Warren Ellis — Writer
John Cassaday — Artist

Laura DePuy and David Baron— Colorists
Ryan Cline, Bill O'Neil and Mike Heisler — Letterers

John Layman — Editor
Alex Sinclair, John Cassaday, and Ed Roeder— Logo and Book Design

PLANETARY created by Warren Ellis and John Cassaday

PLANETARY: THE FOURTH MAN Published by WildStorm Productions, 888 Prospect St, Suite 240. La Jolla, CA 92037. Cover, design pages, and compilation © 2001 WildStorm Productions. WildStorm Universe, its logo, Planetary, and all related characters and elements are trademarks of DC Comics. All Rights Reserved.

Originally published in single magazine format as PLANETARY #7-#12. Copyright © 2000, 2001 WildStorm Productions, an imprint of DC Comics. Printed on recyclable paper. WildStorm does not read or accept unsolicited submissions of ideas, stories or artwork. Printed in Canada. THIRD PRINTING.

DC Comics, a Warner Bros. Entertainment Company.

ISBN: 1-56389-764-4   ISBN-13: 978-1-56389-764-1

THE FOURTH MAN

DEDICATIONS

For Stuart Green, Dave Elliott, Marie Javins, and the memory of Archie Goodwin. Without these four, I wouldn't be writing this. So now you know who to blame. And for Niki and Lili, because they've put up with me in the long trip from there to here.
—Warren

During the year in which this art was built, I experienced a great spectrum of personal peaks. Page for page, this book will always remind me of that year and its towering highs and abysmal lows. And what I found along the way. So thank you for it, Lisa. Thank you for it all. I'll miss you.
—John

JIM LEE, Editorial Director   JOHN NEE, VP & General Manager
SCOTT DUNBIER, Group Editor   PAUL LEVITZ, President & Publisher
GEORG BREWER, VP—Design & Retail Product Development   RICHARD BRUNING, Senior VP—Creative Director
PATRICK CALDON, Senior VP—Finance & Operations   CHRIS CARAMALIS, VP—Finance
TERRI CUNNINGHAM, VP—Managing Editor   DAN DiDIO, VP—Editorial
ALISON GILL, VP—Manufacturing   LILLIAN LASERSON, Senior VP & General Counsel   DAVID McKILLIPS, VP—Advertising & Custom Publishing
CHERYL RUBIN, VP—Brand Management   BOB WAYNE, VP—Sales & Marketing

INTRODUCTION BY Joss Whedon

Planetary haunts me.

It haunts me like a dark, low-budget science fiction movie from the fifties, seen on a black and white TV when I was still too young to deal with it. It haunts me like a visionary short story from those pocket-sized magazines with words like Amazing, Astounding or Asimov on the cover. Like a history class that's so good that for a moment you realize people actually lived that stuff, and you're right there with them. Like a Leone western. Like James Bond, if he were actually as cool as we remember him.

Look at the covers. The logo. No two alike. Every issue its own short, dazzling tale that would bind the reader even if they had no idea it was part of a larger whole. I first picked it up at issue #8, the second chapter of this volume. I was stunned by the imagination, the darkness, the scope of the thing. Plus, hey, giant ants. Going back and buying the first seven issues was an instant necessity, as was waiting droolingly for every issue since. What kept blowing me away was how different each piece was. There was more imagination and originality in every issue of Planetary than in practically any movie you're gonna see this year. Warren Ellis draws inspiration from so many cultural wellsprings that his work truly does become a sort of history of the twentieth century as it exists in popular fiction. But this is no mere pastiche — Ellis both subverts and elevates the elements he takes, making them fit perfectly his own epic vision. No one who loves comics can get through issue #10, "Magic and Loss," without a true thrill of childlike dread.

Ellis's love of literature and history, filtered through his own strange vision, puts him alongside contemporary Alan Moore in more than just quality. One could easily see their universes entwined — Tom Strong and perhaps Miss Mina Murray bumping into Elijah Snow and Jenny Sparks of The Authority. While so many comics are rebooting, Ultimating and Year One-ing themselves into a masturbatory frenzy, these two are creating universes as rich and strange as any we could hope to encounter; eerily familiar and total-ly new. The two stand right now as the pillars of modern comics. (Or possibly the "intimidating British guys with intense facial hair of modern comics," but "pillars" is easier to say.) What separates them is that while Moore's pages overflow with visual information, his panels crammed with explosions of life and lore, Ellis gives us a sparer, more cinematic frame. He takes his time. He waits.

Then the giant ants.

Or the rocket, the well of ghosts, the pattern of ice in a grassy park. His sense of pace, of space, is truly epic. He is aided in this by the extraordinary John Cassaday. Capable of extreme detail but never giving more information than needed for the moment, Casssaday is the perfect match for Ellis' vision. Ellis clearly wants to let the visuals tell his story (another nearly lost art in comics), and Cassaday rewards us with breathtaking vistas alternating with quiet, wry moments of humanity. He puts us in giant alien chambers, and we are there, puts us up close in moments of appalling violence, and we are there. He captures. Plus, Jakita Wagner: wicked hot.

Jakita's hotness aside, it's really Elijah Snow that this book belongs to. It's in this second volume that pieces of the puzzle begin to come together, that Elijah does more than just excavate. The whole begins to take shape and what would have been perfectly fine as an unrelated series of short stories begins to reveal itself as something much more complex and rewarding. Snow is a great character to walk this world with. The "creepy old goat," as one bystander calls him, is a man who's done too little, seen too much, and finally had enough. He's terminally cranky, and I admire that in a hero.

So go with him. Go back for a second trip through the warped scape Ellis and Cassaday have woven, and see if it doesn't haunt you a little bit. The game's afoot. Enjoy.

Joss Whedon
1/1/01

Joss Whedon is the acclaimed creator of Buffy The Vampire Slayer.

PLANETARY

ELLIS • CASSADAY • BARON

unwavering faith, a
gular piety towards
es a generation the
ound for all that apper-
the beauty of the courts
ord, an imagination
with the glories of the
combined in impelling
t of this memoir to
r his heart and soul
ire for the restoration
gotten faith and for
l in the land of its
agnificence in art and
re.

JACK CARTER'S DEAD.

GOOD.

WHO'S JACK CARTER?

OLD FRIEND OF OURS. HAD SERIOUS CONNECTIONS IN THE OCCULT UNDERGROUND. REAL PLAYER IN THE EIGHTIES.

THE WORD, SNOW, IS SCUMBAG.

HE WAS NOT.

WHATEVER. I'M BIASED. I WASN'T SLEEPING WITH HIM, AFTER ALL.

COMING TO THE FUNERAL?

"To Be In England, In The Summertime"
a tale of the planetary

WARREN ELLIS ~ THE SCRIBE
JOHN CASSADAY ~ THE ILLUSTRATOR
DAVID BARON ~ HUES AND PIGMENTS
with thanks to Laura DePuy
RYAN CLINE ~ CALLIGRAPHY
JOHN LAYMAN ~ THE SPONSOR

WHAT WAS HE LIKE?

JACK CARTER?

JACK WAS...

...JACK WAS EVERYTHING YOU WANTED LONDON TO BE.

YOU KNOW WHAT THEY SAY; IF YOU'RE TIRED OF LONDON, YOU'RE TIRED OF LIFE.

FOR ME, JACK CARTER *WAS* LONDON.

HE WAS FUNNY AND SMART AND MYSTERIOUS AND SEXY AND SCARY...

ALL RIGHT, SQUIRE?

YOU COULD NEVER GET TIRED OF HIM.

AND I'LL MISS HIM TERRIBLY.

YOU'RE NEVER WHAT I EXPECT, JAKITA.

HE WAS OUR WINDOW ON ENGLAND IN THE EIGHTIES. LOTS OF STRANGE STUFF WENT ON HERE. EVEN WITHOUT THE COSTUMED STUFF.

COSTUMED? THERE WERE SUPERHEROES IN ENGLAND?

SURE. JENNY SPARKS RAN A TEAM HERE IN THE SIXTIES, AND AGAIN IN THE EIGHTIES. ALL WENT TO HELL, OF COURSE.

I THINK THERE WERE SOME HOLDOVERS FROM THAT, TOO -- ONE OR TWO PEOPLE WANTING "TO DO IT RIGHT."

YOU CAN NEVER QUITE GET RID OF ALL THE "TRADITIONALISTS," NO MATTER HOW MANY CONDOMS YOU SELL.

JACK LET US IN ON THAT, AND ALL THE OTHER STUFF....

ONE OF THESE DAYS YOU PAINS IN THE BACKSIDE WILL SPEAK A COMPLETE SENTENCE THAT I DON'T HAVE TO ASK ANOTHER DAMN QUESTION ABOUT...

...WHAT "OTHER STUFF"?

WELL...

...COME AND MEET THEM.

THERE'S THE SHIFTING MAN; FELL OUT OF A SHIFTDOOR WEARING SOME KIND OF BLEED-SUIT IN '85...

...CURRENT INCARNATION OF THE FOREST DEITY...THEY'VE BEEN BRITISH-BASED SINCE THE TIME OF ROBIN HOOD, APPARENTLY...

NONE OF THEM LOOK EXACTLY HAPPY, EVEN FOR A FUNERAL...

THEY'RE EIGHTIES PEOPLE.

JACK ALWAYS SAID IT WAS DIFFICULT FOR US AMERICANS TO UNDERSTAND WHAT IT WAS REALLY LIKE HERE IN THE DARKEST PARTS OF THE EIGHTIES.

WE HAD A DODDERY OLD PRESIDENT WHO TALKED ABOUT THE END OF THE WORLD A LITTLE TOO OFTEN AND WAS BEING RUN BY THE WRONG PEOPLE.

BUT THEY HAD A PRIME MINISTER WHO WAS GENUINELY MAD.

YOU KNOW THERE WERE EVEN FEMINISTS AND WOMEN'S STUDIES THEORISTS WHO DENIED SHE WAS EVEN REALLY A WOMAN ANYMORE, SHE WAS SO FAR OUT OF HER TREE?

SHE WANTED CONCENTRATION CAMPS FOR AIDS VICTIMS, WANTED TO ERADICATE HOMOSEXUALITY EVEN AS AN ABSTRACT CONCEPT, MADE POOR PEOPLE CHOOSE BETWEEN EATING AND KEEPING THEIR VOTE...

...RAN THE MOST SHAMELESS VOTE-GRABBING ARTIFICIAL WAR SCAM IN FIFTY YEARS...

ENGLAND WAS A SCARY PLACE. NO WONDER IT PRODUCED A SCARY CULTURE.

I DUNNO. MAYBE IT'S ME, MAYBE IT'S TEN YEARS DIFFERENCE BETWEEN HERE AND THE CULTURE THAT PRODUCED THEM, BUT...

...DON'T THEY LOOK FAINTLY RIDICULOUS?

AH, PROBABLY. WHAT DOESN'T LOOK FUNNY, TEN YEARS LATER? PEOPLE BOUGHT FLARES, REMEMBER.

TWICE.

THE IMPORTANT THING IS HOW THEY DEALT WITH THE TIME. AND IT WAS NOT THE BEST OF TIMES. JACK TOLD ME A STORY:

1987

SOME NIGHTS, IT NEVER SEEMS
TO GET PROPERLY DARK IN LONDON.
CLOUD COMES OVER AND BLANKETS
THE TOWN, AND THE ORANGE GLOW
OF THE STREETLIGHTS SUFFUSES
IT, SO THAT LONDON LOOKS LIKE
IT'S TRAPPED IN AMBER, AND US
WITH IT. AND WE ALL LOOK UP
AND NOD LIKE OUR MUMS AND DADS
AND PARROT THE OLD "WELL, IT'D
BE COLD WITHOUT THAT CLOUD
COVER," AND DON'T FOR A MINUTE
THINK ABOUT BEING SEALED IN
LONDON WITH NO ESCAPE.

THE SKY WAS BLACK AND
ORANGE WHEN I LEFT MAD
LINDSAY'S GAFF ABOVE THE
SHOE SHOP IN CARNABY STREET.
I DIDN'T LOOK BACK. I KNEW
SHE'D HAVE HER CHOPS PRESSED
TO THE WINDOW, SCREAMING HER
GUTS OUT AND PULLING WEIRD
FACES. SEALED IN BRICK AND
GLASS. THERE WAS A RIPPLING
SOUND, LIKE WAVES BREAKING,
JUST ABOUT AUDIBLE FROM HERE
ABOVE THE TAXIS. IT WAS HER
OWN STUPID FAULT. EVIL MOO.
I DID ME ZIP UP INDISCREETLY
IN FRONT OF A BLOKE OF THREE
HUNDRED COLLECTING FOR THE
SALVATION ARMY AND MADE HIM
GIVE ME TWENTY QUID BEFORE
ANGLING OFF CARNABY INTO BEAK
STREET, WALKING UP INTO
SOHO'S TANGLES.

CHRISTMAS NEVER DOES BUGGER ALL TO SOHO. IT'S GREY AND DOOMED AND HOPELESS AND LIFE-SUCKING ALL YEAR ROUND. EVEN THE BEAUTIFUL GIRLS, NEW TO THE LIFE, EAGER OR CALCULATING, ADD TO THE MISERY BY IMPLICATION. YOU KNOW HOW THEIR STORIES WILL END.

I WAS JUST FANCYING A PINT AT THE COACH AND HORSES WHEN I SAW A MAN WHO WASN'T THERE.

OH, FOR GOD'S SAKE.

YOU CAN BLOODY SEE ME, CAN'T YOU?

THIS PROSTITUTE... YOU'RE TELLING ME SHE'S PREGNANT?

PREGNANT WITH...

WELL, NO-ONE KNOWS FOR SURE, DO THEY? BUT, YOU KNOW, BETTER SAFE THAN SORRY.

I MEAN, NO-ONE KNOWS WHAT'S BEST FOR US BETTER THAN THE PRIME MINISTER, DO THEY?

I'M JUST A CIVIL SERVANT, GOVERNMENT EMPLOYEE. I JUST DO MY JOB, BECAUSE THEM HIGHER-UP THAN ME, THEY KNOW BETTER, DUN'T THEY?

IT'S BAD ENOUGH I'VE JUST HAD TO DO SOMETHING THOROUGHLY BLOODY ROTTEN TO AN OLD GIRLFRIEND BECAUSE SHE TRIED TO KILL ME AND MOST OF THE PEOPLE I KNOW.

BUT TO BUMP INTO SOME BLOODY TORY CIVIL SERVANT SPOOK OFF TO BUTCHER A COMPLETE STRANGER BECAUSE SHE'S INCONVENIENTLY PREGNANT --

AND BE THANKFUL THAT'S ALL I DO TO YOU, YOU TOERAG.

GREEK st

MEMORIAL SERVICE WITHOUT A BODY. TERRIBLE THING.

IT WAS ONLY A DAMN CREMATION, SNOW.

WHERE ARE WE GOING?

I WANT TO SEE WHERE JACK DIED.

WHY?

GOD, I DON'T KNOW. TO SAY GOODBYE PROPERLY. A CLOSED BOX AND A ROCK DOESN'T CUT IT.

SEE?

CRAP. JAKITA, HE WAS A CON MAN WHO PULLED A SCAM ONCE TOO OFTEN.

NO-ONE LIKED HIM AND EVENTUALLY HE PISSED OFF SOMEONE WHO WASN'T AFRAID OF THE SPOOKY BAD MAGICIAN REP.

RIGHT HERE. SOMEONE JUMPED HIM AND BEAT HIM TO DEATH RIGHT HERE. THAT'S ALL THAT HAPPENED.

THERE'S BEEN MAGIC HERE.

MAGIC'S A MESSY SIGNAL, KIND OF LOOSE AND LOSSY. THERE'S TRACES EVERYWHERE.

YOU CAN *SEE MAGIC?*

MAGIC IS THE CHEAT CODES FOR THE WORLD.

SENDING A SIGNAL TO REALITY'S OPERATING SYSTEM, SEE?

YEAH.

SO YOU'VE HEARD ME TALKING ABOUT CHEAT CODES. THINGS THAT I CAN SAY TO THE COMPUTER THAT ALTER THINGS IN THE GAME ENVIRONMENT.

MAGIC WORDS.

SORT OF. MAGIC'S JUST SIGNAL, JUST INFORMATION, AND THAT PUTS IT IN MY BALLCOURT.

IT'S LIKE... YOU'VE SEEN ME PLAYING COMPUTER GAMES?

JACK!

'ELLO, JAKITA, LOVE. KNEW YOU'D DO RIGHT BY ME.

OH, WELL. PROB'LY TIME I QUIT ANYWAY.

WHY DID YOU FAKE YOUR OWN DEATH? HELL, *HOW?*

WELL, IT WAS FAIRLY BLEEDIN' OBVIOUS THAT CHUMMY THERE FANCIED BEATING ME TO DEATH FOR GOD ONLY KNOWS WHAT REASON...

...AND SINCE I COULD'VE DONE WITHOUT THAT, WELL, I HAD TO PULL A BIT OF A STUNT AND THEN GO UNDERGROUND.

HE DID SEEM A BIT DETERMINED, AFTER ALL.

AND IF THERE'S ONE THING I'VE GOTTEN GOOD AT IN THIRTY-ODD YEARS ABOVE GROUND, IT'S DISAPPEARING.

BUT WHEN YOU TURNED UP, EVERYTHING CHANGED.

I KNEW YOU'D WORK OUT WHAT HAPPENED.

AND SO DRAW THAT TOERAG OUT INTO THE LIGHT.

SO I COULD SORT HIM FOR GOOD.

NOT LIKE I EVER CLAIMED TO BE A ROLE MODEL, AFTER ALL.

THE EIGHTIES ARE LONG OVER. TIME TO MOVE ON.

TIME TO BE SOMEONE ELSE.

THE DAY THE EARTH TURNED SLOWER

a planetary production

written by Warren Ellis
illustrated by John Cassaday
and Laura DePuy in WildStormFX
with special thanks to Wendy Fouts
lettered by Ryan Cline
with John Layman as editor

OH, GOD...

...LOOK AT HER.

SORRY ABOUT THAT.

I KICKED IT A LITTLE TOO HARD.

HAVE FUN?

HELL, YES.

GOT OUR PILOT OUT TOO.

HOW'RE WE DOING, ALLISON?

I NEVER EXPECTED TO BE BACK HERE. I MEAN, I USED TO HAVE NIGHTMARES ABOUT ENDING UP HERE.

DO YOU HAVE ANY IDEA OF WHAT HAPPENED HERE?

ONLY RUMORS.

CITY ZERO WAS, FIRST AND FOREMOST, AN EXPERIMENTAL CONCENTRATION CAMP FOR AMERICAN DISSIDENTS.

THEY NEEDED WARM BODIES FOR WHAT THEY HAD PLANNED. THEY WANTED RID OF ALL US SUPPOSED REDS UNDER THE BED. PERFECT PLAN.

THEY PICKED UP THOSE OF US WHOSE DISAPPEARANCES WERE EXPLAINABLE. THE DRINKERS, THE DOPERS...

...WOMEN WHO SLEPT WITH THE WRONG MEN...

THEY DISAPPEARED US.

BROUGHT US HERE.

WERE QUITE OPEN ABOUT THE FACT THEY COULD DO ANYTHING THEY WANTED TO US.

AND BEGAN TO CHANGE US.

IN HERE.

THIS IS THEATRE A. THIS IS WHERE THEY DRAGGED MY CORPSE. I'M TOLD I WAS STILL WARM WHEN THEY PUT ME ON THE TABLE, STILL LEAKING.

WEIRD. IT ALMOST SEEMS HARMLESS, SEEING IT ALL LIKE THIS.

THE DEVIL'S EMPTY HOUSE.

I REMEMBER THE SMELLS, FIRST. OZONE. BONFIRES.

AND THEN THE LIGHT. IT FLICKERED, FLARED, SENT EVERYTHING MONOCHROME, AND THEN ELECTRIC BLUE, AND THEN FLICKERED AGAIN.

A VOICE SAYING "ATOMICS." SOMETHING ELSE; ATOMIC RAY, ATOMIC PROJECTION, SOMETHING LIKE THAT.

ATOMICS.

I KNEW I'D DIED. I'D FELT THE BULLETS TEAR ME OPEN, RIP ME UP INSIDE.

THEY DON'T TELL YOU THAT, YOU KNOW; THAT YOU CAN FEEL THE BULLETS MOVING INSIDE YOU, BURNING CHANNELS INSIDE YOUR BODY.

YOU ASSUME A FIRING SQUAD DEATH WILL BE QUICK, BUT IT'S NOT. I FINISHED THE SCREAM I STARTED JUST BEFORE I DIED.

THE MAN WHO OPERATED ON ME WAITED PATIENTLY UNTIL I HAD TO BREATHE AGAIN, AND THEN SAID;

MY NAME IS DOCTOR RANDALL DOWLING. CAN YOU UNDERSTAND ME?

I BROUGHT YOU BACK FROM THE DEAD. CAN YOU UNDERSTAND?

DOWLING.

UNREAL.

WHAT YEAR ARE WE TALKING ABOUT HERE? '50? CITY ZERO WAS AN *ARTEMIS* OPERATION? IS THIS WHAT YOU'RE TELLING US?

NO. IT WAS A GOVERNMENT OPERATION. BUT THESE WERE THE EARLY DAYS OF THE MILITARY-INDUSTRIAL COMPLEX, AS WELL AS OF THE COMPLEX POST-WAR WEB OF SPOOKSHOWS.

THERE WAS A WOMAN HERE. YOUNG, ASIAN.

SHE REPRESENTED SOMETHING CALLED THE HARK CORPORATION.

HOW LONG?

SHE SAID.

SHE WASN'T TALKING TO ME, OF COURSE. SHE WAS TALKING TO DOWLING. I GOT THE IMPRESSION SHE DIDN'T LIKE HIM, OR CITY ZERO.

I GOT THE FEELING THAT IT WAS ALL BELOW HER, BUT NECESSARY. EXPEDIENT. ANYWAY, HE SAID

AS DISCUSSED, MISS HARK.

THIS WOMAN HAS A RADIOACTIVE HALF-LIFE OF FIFTY YEARS.

IT WASN'T JUST ME, OF COURSE.

THEY DID SOMETHING TO ALL OF US.

ALL OF US THAT WERE STRONG ENOUGH TO WITHSTAND THE PROCEDURES, ANYWAY.

THE SCREENWRITER. PACIFIST. COMMUNIST. A DRINKER.

BEGGING THE SOLDIERS TO SHOOT HIM AS HE MOVED IN AND OUT OF VISIBILITY.

HE WOULD HAVE TRIED TO KILL HIMSELF, BUT HE'D GONE BLIND FROM INVISIBILITY, AND THE PAIN WAS CRIPPLING HIM...

THE DISGRACED OFFICER.

WE HEARD HIS BONES STRETCHING FROM BEYOND THE COMPOUND, WHEN THEY PUT THE TREATMENT ON HIM.

I DEVELOPED A LOVER IN THE CITY MEDICAL CORPS. HE SAID THAT THE AUTOPSY REVEALED A NORMAL-SIZED BRAIN HANGING IN A WEB OF NERVE TISSUE LIKE CABLES IN A SKULL SEVERAL FEET ACROSS.

AT NIGHT,
ATOMIC DOGS PROWLED
THE COMPOUND. IN THE DISTANCE, WE
COULD ALWAYS HEAR THE ANTS, LOCKED
IN THEIR FLEXING CAGES AT THE EDGE
OF THE CITY, SHRIEKING LIKE
STARVING BABIES...

WE WOULD TRY
TO SLEEP, CRAMMED
INTO UNISEX BARRACKS,
BUT IT WAS SO
HARD...

THERE WAS A MAN WHOSE
BRAIN HAD BEEN REPLACED BY AN
"ATOMIC SNOWFLAKE FIELD," WHO WAS
CHANNELING THE CONSCIOUSNESS OF
SOMEONE ON ANOTHER PLANET, WHO
WOULD WHISPER OBSCENITIES
ALL NIGHT LONG, NEVER
REPEATING HIMSELF...

THEY LAUGHED TO LOOK AT US, THE SOLDIERS AND EVERYONE ELSE WITHOUT THE RIGHT NEED-TO-KNOW.

WE WERE THE BIG JOKE; DIRTY REDS BEING USED AS GUINEA PIGS FOR THE SPECIAL ANTI-RED SUPER-ARMY TO COME.

BUT THE ACTUAL JOKE WAS EVEN WORSE.

THERE WAS NO REAL "RED THREAT." THEY WERE AS AFRAID OF US AS WE WERE OF THEM.

THE PEOPLE WHO BUILT CITY ZERO KNEW IT. THAT'S NOT WHY THEY BUILT CITY ZERO.

THE "RED THREAT" ANGLE JUST GOT THEM THE INITIAL FUNDING AND THE SECRECY THEY NEEDED.

CITY ZERO WAS SIMPLY ABOUT TESTING THE HUMAN BODY TO THE LIMITS OF THE AVAILABLE TECHNOLOGY.

IT WAS ABOUT SEEING WHAT THEY COULD GET AWAY WITH DOING TO US.

CAN WE GO OUTSIDE?

FOR ME, PERSONALLY, I CAN'T ALWAYS BE ANGRY AT THEM. YOU NEVER GET TIRED OF LOOKING AT THE STARS, DO YOU, MISTER SNOW?

AND I'VE SEEN THEM A LOT MORE THAN I OTHERWISE MIGHT.

BUT WHAT THEY DID TO EVERYONE ELSE...

CITY ZERO WAS LEFT VERY QUICKLY. DR. DOWLING HAD MORE THAN ONE CHANGE OF FORTUNE BEFORE THE END OF THE DECADE.

SOME OF THE INFORMATION IS STILL HERE. TRAPPED IN MACHINES, BURIED IN ABANDONED BOOKS.

FOR ALL THEIR SAKES. FOR OUR SAKE. USE IT.

I COULD HAVE DONE THIS A WHILE AGO. BUT I'M A COWARD. I WANTED TO LIVE FOR AS LONG AS I COULD, YOU SEE?

IT WAS ONLY HALF A LIFE, BUT I WANTED IT.

RADIOACTIVE HALF-LIFE OF FIFTY YEARS.

TIME'S UP.

I'M SO GLAD I MET YOU.

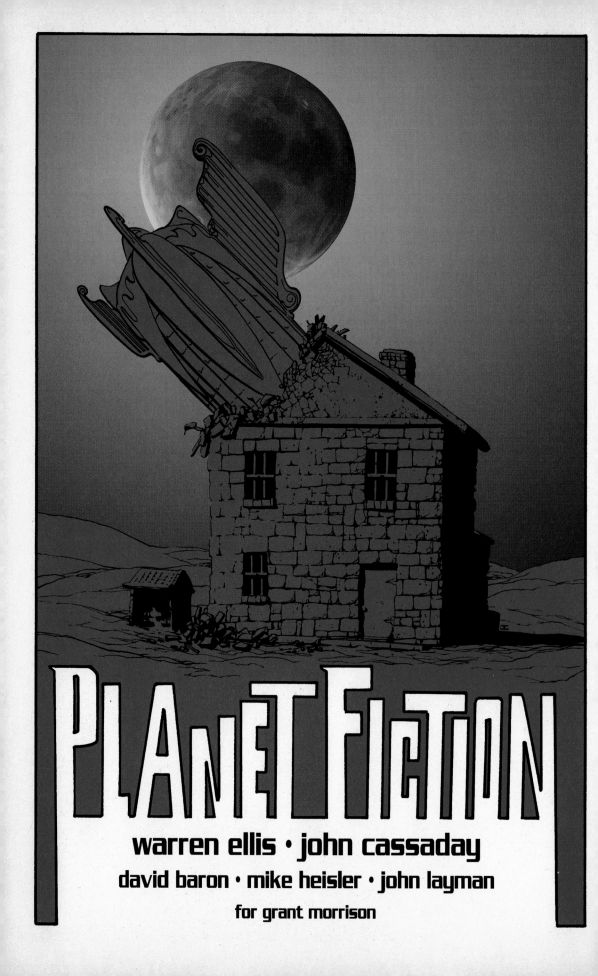

PLANET FICTION

warren ellis · john cassaday

david baron · mike heisler · john layman

for grant morrison

TOO EASY. WE'RE GOOD, BUT NOT THIS GOOD. WE KNOW THERE'S A STRENGTH OF TWO THOUSAND ON THIS SITE. DRUMS, TALK TO ME.

DATA FLOW'S GETTING SLUGGISH IN HERE. LOOKS LIKE THEY'VE GOT A PARTIAL POWER OUTAGE IN THE SITE'S CENTRAL SECTIONS.

AMBROSE?

NOTHING TO DO WITH ME. MY REALITY DISTORTION FIELD IS UNPREDICTABLE, BUT IT AIN'T PUTTING OUT LIGHTS WITHOUT ME KNOWING.

IN WHICH CASE, THIS IS HORRIBLY BAD NEWS.

THEIR RETRIEVAL OP'S GONE BAD ALREADY. AND WHATEVER THEY PULLED OUT OF PLANET FICTION COULD ALREADY BE LOOSE.

WHICH MEANS THAT YOUR TWO THOUSAND SOLDIERS ARE PROBABLY FORMED UP AROUND THE CENTRAL SECTIONS.

KEEP YOUR HEAD DOWN, DRUMS.

THIS IS GOING TO GET DAMN UGLY.

I KNEW IT WAS GOING TO GET UGLY WHEN I TAPPED THEIR COMMS.

FOUR CONFIRMED OCCUPANTS OF THE EXPLORATION VESSEL.

AND THEY ONLY SENT THREE PEOPLE IN.

EMERGENCY GENERATOR'S DOWN TOO

WHERE ARE THE DAMN TORCHES?

BATTERY-DRIVEN SPOTLIGHTS IN THE STORE ON GREEN CORRIDOR

OH MY GOD

GET SOME LIGHT IN THERE. DO IT NOW.

THEY CAN'T HEAR YOU, WE'VE LOST POWER TO COMMS.

I CAN SEE SOMETHING ELSE DOWN THERE...

GOD, DO YOU SMELL THAT? WHAT IS THAT?

I CAN HEAR SOMETHING...NOT QUITE MUSIC...

OH, NO...

GET UPSTAIRS TO THE CONTROL ROOM. TELL HORNE --

-- I COUNT THREE BODIES IN HERE, ALL DEAD, TWO MUTILATED.

WE'RE LIVING INSIDE A SCIENCE FICTION MOVIE.

THE BLACK GUY ALWAYS DIES IN SCIENCE FICTION MOVIES.

TELL... THE FOURTH MAN...

...I ALWAYS... DID THE BEST... POSSIBLE JOB...

I KNOW, BABY. I KNOW.

IN 1997, THE FOURTH MAN WAS MISSING IN ACTION.

ELIJAH SNOW HAS NEVER HEARD OF AMBROSE CHASE.

JAKITA WAGNER WAS ALREADY A MEMBER OF PLANETARY
WHEN AMBROSE CHASE BECAME THE THIRD MAN.

THE FOURTH INDIVIDUAL BROUGHT BACK FROM THE
SAMPLE RETURN MISSION IS STILL AT LARGE.

planetary

MAGIC & LOSS

WARREN ELLIS writer
JOHN CASSADAY artist
LAURA DePUY and
DAVID BARON colorists

RYAN CLINE letterer
JOHN LAYMAN editor
PLANETARY created by
warren ellis & john cassaday

ON NIGHTS LIKE THIS, AMERICA LOOKS CLOSE ENOUGH TO TOUCH. THE LAMPS OF ITS TANGLES OF ROADS, ITS CONSTELLATIONS OF HOUSES.

AND THEY CAN'T SEE US.

NOT UNTIL THEY'RE READY. THEY MUST NOT EVEN KNOW WE'RE HERE.

WE'VE BEEN OVER THIS, MOTHER.

I CAN'T TELL THEM WHERE THE ISLAND IS, OR EVEN HOW IT COMES TO BE THAT THEY HAVE NEVER BEEN ABLE TO PERCEIVE THE ISLAND.

I JUST HAVE TO TELL THEM IT'S HERE, TELL THEM WHAT WE HAVE...

...EXPLAIN TO THE COUNTRY WITH THE GREAT PHALLIC ROCKETS THAT A SECRET FEMALE SOCIETY OFF THEIR SHORE IS ABOUT SIX HUNDRED YEARS AHEAD OF THEM.

OH, THOSE SILLY ROCKETS. IT'S THOSE THAT MADE UP MY MIND.

THEIR STUPID POLITICS ARE FORCING MOON-TRAVEL AT LEAST SIX YEARS TOO EARLY FOR THEM. AND THEY WON'T GO BACK, ONCE THEY'VE ACHIEVED IT.

NO. THE TIME IS RIGHT.

YOU NEED TO GO TO THEIR WORLD.

PREPARE THEM FOR THE REVELATION OF THE ISLAND. BRING THEM NEWS OF A BETTER WAY TO LIVE.

COLD WORLD

by **WARREN ELLIS**

and **JOHN CASSADAY**

with **LAURA DEPUY**

and **BILL O'NEIL**

as produced by **JOHN LAYMAN**

Planetary created by
Warren Ellis and John Cassaday

GOT A LIGHT?

IT'S A GAZER.

FOCUSED REACTIONLESS GRAVITY BEAM. WOULD'VE PUNCHED A HOLE THROUGH YOUR BRAIN BIG ENOUGH TO SPIT THROUGH.

SHE USED IT ON A GIRLFRIEND OF MINE IN MARRAKESH IN '67.

I WAS TRYING TO WORK OUT HOW TO STEAL HER PLANE.

WITHOUT THE PLANE, YOU SEE, SHE COULDN'T GET AWAY AND I COULD MAKE SURE SHE WAS ARRESTED OR SHOT. EITHER WAY, I GOT A LITTLE REVENGE.

I'M ELIJAH SNOW.

STONE.

JOHN STONE.

AGENT OF S.T.O.R.M.

KAZAKHSTAN.

GIVE ME A BEER. GIVE THIS OLD MAN A BEER, TOO.

HELLO, ELIJAH.

BEEN A WHILE.

WHAT IS THIS PLACE?

IT'S VERY SECRET. YOU WANTED PRIVACY.

IT'S CALLED THE LAST SHOT.

THERE'S A TEAM OF ROGUE EX-SOVIET NUCLEAR TECHNICIANS HOLED UP NEARBY.

ATTACHED TO THE SAME RESEARCH TEAM THAT ESTABLISHED THAT THE HUMAN SOUL IS AN ELECTROMAGNETIC FIELD.

THEY SAY THEY ALSO FOUND OUT WHERE SOULS GO.

THAT HEAVEN AND HELL ARE NOTHING BUT SIEGE ENGINES SET IN A CONSTANT TUG-OF-WAR AGAINST EACH OTHER, AND SOULS PROVIDE THE COAL.

THIS IS THE PLACE WHERE THE AFTERLIFE GETS CHEATED.

ELECTRO-MAGNETIC FIELDS, YOU SEE, GET TERMINALLY DISRUPTED BY NUCLEAR EXPLOSIONS.

THEY HAVE THEIR LAST DRINK AND THEIR PHOTO TAKEN HERE, AND THEN GO TO BE STRAPPED TO AN UNDERGROUND NUCLEAR TEST DEVICE.

TO THE TRIUMPHANT DEAD.

THAT'S SOMETHING WORTH TOASTING.

DAMNIT.

I'VE GOT HOLES IN MY MEMORY YOU COULD THROW A DAMN NUKE THROUGH.

OKAY. *YES,* I KNOW OF WILLIAM LEATHER.

WHY?

I MET HIM RECENTLY.

SO I HEARD. THE INTEL COMMUNITY HAD A FIT.

JUST MARCH RIGHT INTO THE MAIN LAB OF THE FOUR MOST FRIGHTENING PEOPLE ON EARTH AND TRASH THE PLACE. EVERYONE WISHES THEY'D THOUGHT OF IT.

HE KNEW ME. KNEW ME OF OLD. AND I'D NEVER MET HIM BEFORE THAT NIGHT.

HE SAID SOMETHING TO ME.

DO YOU REALLY NOT REMEMBER US?

WHO BENEFITS FROM YOUR LACK OF MEMORY?

WHO KNOWS THE SECRET HISTORY OF ELIJAH SNOW?

WHAT ARE YOUR TEAMMATES NOT TELLING YOU?

YOU'RE THE BEST AND ONLY EXPERT ON SECRETS I KNOW, JOHN.

HELP.

THINK ABOUT WHAT LEATHER SAID.

WHO BENEFITS FROM YOUR LACK OF MEMORY?

HE DOES.

HE'S MET YOU BEFORE. HE KNOWS YOU. BUT YOU DON'T KNOW HIM.

THEREFORE, *HE* BENEFITS. HE HAS YOU AT A DIS-ADVANTAGE.

I'VE BEEN PLAYING MINDGAMES LIKE THIS SINCE O.S.S. HELL, I'VE BEEN PLAYING THEM SINCE BEFORE THE WORD WAS INVENTED.

I WAS ON THE NAUTILUS?

WHY WOULD THEY NOT WANT ME TO KNOW I WAS ON THE NAUTILUS?

SOMEONE'S RUNNING A GAME ON YOU, ELIJAH.

SAME SORT OF GAME I RAN IN THE SEVENTIES WHEN I LEFT S.T.O.R.M. TO HEAD UP THE UNREAL SANCTION FORCE.

SOMEONE'S BUILT YOU A VIRTUAL WORLD. A SCAFFOLD OF LIES STRONG ENOUGH TO HOLD UNDER PRESSURE.

WHY? BECAUSE HE AND HIS HAVE KNOWN YOU A WHILE. THEY KNOW YOU'RE NOT ON THEIR SIDE.

SO NOW THEY GET TO CONSTANTLY WRONG-FOOT YOU, KNOCK YOU OFF GUARD, KEEP YOU DISTRACTED.

ONLY ONE PROBLEM WITH THAT SCENARIO.

WHAT?

THEY'RE THE FOUR. THEY COULD JUST KILL YOU. THEY COULD JUST KILL PLANETARY.

HELL, THEY COULD KILL HALF AMERICA BEFORE LUNCH IF THEY FELT LIKE IT. AND GET AWAY WITH IT.

IT'S NOT JUST "WHY WOULD THEY RUN A GAME ON YOU?" IT'S ALSO "WHY WOULD THEY NOT JUST KILL YOU?"

YOU REMEMBER ME, YOU DON'T REMEMBER THE NAUTILUS, BUT YOU DETECT NO FLAW. VERY ELEGANT JOB THEY DID ON YOU.

HOW MUCH DO YOU REMEMBER ABOUT YOUR LIFE?

I CAN GET UP, I CAN DO IT --

YOU'RE SHAKING LIKE A LEAF.

STRESS AND SHOCK. WOULD PROBABLY BE WORSE IF I HADN'T HAD A BEER, HEH...

GIVE ME A CIGARETTE, FOR GOD'S SAKE.

HOW MUCH HAS COME BACK?

NOT ALL OF IT, NOT NEARLY ALL OF IT, BUT ENOUGH THAT I KNOW MORE IS MISSING, IF YOU SEE WHAT I MEAN.

YOU WERE RIGHT. THE FOUR DID IT TO ME.

STRUCTURE OF MEMORY BLOCKS. "IT'S A GAME, MR. SNOW." NO IDEA WHY.

BY THE WAY, KEEP YOURSELF AVAILABLE FOR INTERVIEW, JOHN.

I WANT TO KNOW WHY YOU'RE WORKING FOR ANNA HARK.

GLAD YOU'RE BACK, ELIJAH.

I'LL BET.

IT GETS BETTER.

MEMORY CLOUD

by **Warren Ellis**
and **John Cassaday**
with **Laura DePuy**
Lettered by **Bill O'Neil**
Edited by **John Layman**
Planetary created by Warren Ellis and John Cassaday

ELIJAH?

COME IN.

SIT DOWN.

I DON'T KNOW WHY YOU CALLED US IN HERE, BUT WE REALLY NEED TO TALK ABOUT YOUR USE OF THE HELICOPTERS, AND WE SHOULD POSTPONE --

SIT DOWN.

-- ANY OTHER BUSINESS UNTIL WE'VE STRAIGHTENED OUT THE PROTOCOL ON BORROWING EXPENSIVE EQUIPMENT AND --

SIDDOWN.

THIS IS GETTING VERY WEIRD, SNOW...

SHUT UP, DRUMS.

...JUST SAYING, MAN, THIS IS KIND OF DISTURBING, YOU MUTTERING AWAY IN THE DARK...

DRUMS.

SHUT UP AND LET ME GET THIS DONE OR I'LL FREEZE EVERY DROP OF FLUID IN YOUR SCROTUM SOLID.

FOR A START.

NOW ISN'T THAT INTERESTING.

DRUMS HERE HAS TREATED ME AS A JOKE -- AN OLD JOKE AT THAT -- FROM THE MINUTE I GOT HERE.

AND NOW HE'S SCARED TO DEATH OF ME.

WHY IS THAT, DO YOU THINK?

LET'S SEE NOW.

SINCE YOU'RE SUDDENLY DOING AS YOU'RE TOLD.

DO YOU KNOW WHAT A PLANETARY GUIDE IS?

IT'S OKAY, DRUMS.

IT'S A BOOK --

I ASKED *HIM.*

IT'S A BOOK THAT'S BEEN PUBLISHED UNDERGROUND ANNUALLY SINCE 1925.

AND WHO WRITES IT, DRUMS?

WHO WRITES IT?

YOU DO.

I DO.

AND YET I'VE SPENT THE LAST SEVERAL YEARS UNABLE TO REMEMBER THAT I'VE BEEN WRITING THE PLANETARY GUIDE SINCE 1925.

STRANGE, ISN'T IT?

I REMEMBER GUNNING DOWN THE DEPLOYMENT EGGS OF ALIEN ORGANIC WAR-AUTOMATA IN JUDGEMENT, RHODE ISLAND IN JANUARY OF 1931 LIKE IT WAS YESTERDAY.

BUT I DIDN'T REMEMBER WRITING IT UP FOR THE '31 PLANETARY GUIDE UNTIL LAST NIGHT.

WHY IS THAT, DO YOU THINK?

WHY ARE YOU LEANING ON HIM, ELIJAH?

I KNOW I CAN'T SLAP YOU AROUND. I KNOW I *CAN* SLAP *HIM* AROUND.

ALL RIGHT, THEN.

ALL RIGHT.

YOU CREATED THE PLANETARY GUIDE IN 1925.

THAT'S WHY YOU WERE IN JUDGEMENT IN 1931.

BUT YOU REMEMBER IT AS SIMPLY HAVING BEEN INVOLVED IN SOME WEIRD STUFF SINCE YOU WERE A KID AND BEING INVITED OUT TO JUDGEMENT FOR YOUR EXPERIENCE, RIGHT?

RIGHT.

SO THE QUESTION IS WHY DIDN'T THEY WANT ME TO REMEMBER THE PLANETARY GUIDE?

I THINK I KNOW.

YOU'RE GETTING FRIGHTENED NOW, AREN'T YOU?

YOU'RE WONDERING HOW MUCH I REMEMBER, AND HOW MUCH TROUBLE IT COULD CAUSE.

I REMEMBER ALL KINDS OF THINGS.

OH, TELL ME YOU DON'T REMEMBER *THAT*...

WHAT DO YOU REMEMBER, ELIJAH?

I KNEW SHERLOCK HOLMES.

TO BE A *DETECTIVE*, THEN, MY BOY?

VERY WELL. I CAN INSTRUCT YOU IN MY METHODS. THE FACT THAT YOU FOUND ME PROVES YOUR POTENTIAL.

TO WORK, THEN. FOR THIS IS YOUR CENTURY, AND IT NEEDS YOU.

I KNEW WHAT WAS BENEATH THE SKIN OF THE WORLD, EVEN THEN. BUT I NEEDED TO KNOW WHAT TO LOOK FOR AND HOW TO LOOK FOR IT.

EVEN THEN, I DIDN'T WRITE THE FIRST PLANETARY GUIDE UNTIL I HAD A SERIOUS SPONSOR. THAT WAS IN 1925.

BY THE WAY.

I REMEMBER WHO THE FOURTH MAN IS.

ELIJAH, WHERE THE HELL ARE YOU GOING?

TALK TO ME, DAMNIT!

I'M GOING IN HERE.

BY THE WAY: I WANT A FILE OPENED UP ON JOHN STONE.

I DON'T BELIEVE FOR A MINUTE THAT MY QUESTIONING THE STRUCTURE OF MY MEMORY BLOCKS WAS ALL IT TOOK TO BEGIN THEIR DISSOLUTION.

WHO'S JOHN STONE?

JOHN STONE IS THE WORLD'S OLDEST AND GREATEST SECRET AGENT.

HE PRETTY MUCH SINGLE-HANDEDLY INVENTED PSYCHOLOGICAL OPERATIONS, TOO.

HE'S WORKING FOR ANNA HARK. I REMEMBERED THAT.

SO IF HE'S WORKING FOR ANNA HARK, WHY WASN'T HE SENT IN TO INVESTIGATE THE BOMBING OF THE HARK CORPORATION BUILDING UNDER WHICH WE FOUND THE GATE TO THE BURIED SHIFTSHIP?

WHY SEND IN JAMES WILDER, THE COMPANY'S PRIVATE INVESTIGATOR, IF YOU HAVE JOHN STONE?

AND, AND, AND WHEN WERE YOU GOING TO TELL ME THIS?

NEVER. YOU *WEREN'T SUPPOSED TO REMEMBER.* YOU DIDN'T REMEMBER *JACK CARTER*, DAMNIT, WHY SHOULD YOU REMEMBER *AMBROSE?*

I REMEMBER WHEN WE WERE GOING TO JACK'S FUNERAL, AND YOU JUST SAID SOMETHING STUPID, AND I REMEMBER LOOKING AT YOU AND THINKING

WHY DON'T YOU REMEMBER?

BUT THIS HASN'T GOT ANYTHING TO DO WITH ANYTHING.

ELIJAH, THEY SAID THEY'D KILL YOU IF YOU STARTED REMEMBERING.

NO THEY DIDN'T.

THEY SAID THEY'D KILL *YOU* UNLESS I SUBMITTED TO THE MEMORY BLOCKS AND WENT AND HID.

THEY SAID THEY'D KILL *YOU.*

BUT YOU CAME AND FOUND ME ANYWAY.

AND WE'VE BEEN POKING AND PRODDING AT YOU TO GET THE OLD ELIJAH BACK WITHOUT THE MEMORY BLOCKS LOOSENING. WE ADMIT IT.

BUT NOW THE BLOCKS HAVE STARTED TO BREAK UP, WE'RE ALL IN IT DEEP.

IT'S A GAME, MISTER SNOW.

BUT, YOU SEE, YOU AND YOUR PEOPLE ARE JUST A LITTLE TOO GOOD AT IT.

IF YOU'RE NOT CAREFUL, YOU MAY GRADUATE FROM AMUSING PEST TO SERIOUS ANNOYANCE.

AND WE CAN'T HAVE THAT.

SO HERE ARE THE RULES:

YOU SUBMIT TO THE PLACING OF A SEQUENCE OF BLOCKS IN YOUR MEMORY. JUST ENOUGH TO PREVENT YOU FROM BEING QUITE SO USEFUL.

AND GO AWAY. GO AND HIDE.

OR I KILL YOUR TEAM.

WE ARE OLD AND POWERFUL AND BORE EASILY. WE ENJOY THE GAME PLANETARY REPRESENTS.

BUT WE CANNOT ALLOW OURSELVES TO LOSE, MISTER SNOW.

SO? SAY, "YES, Dr. DOWLING."

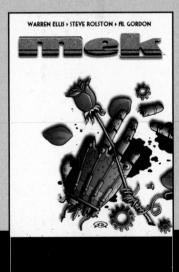

WARREN ELLIS has killed over forty people in single combat over the last two years. Eight of them died by Ellis' bare hands and teeth. So let's have no more smart comments about the English and their bad teeth. He ripped out their throats and bit their hearts in half. That takes good teeth. Hearts are hard. Dense and chewy. You couldn't do it. No. Warren Ellis lives in England with his girlfriend and daughter. And they could bite your hearts in half too.

JOHN CASSADAY has a Venus/Jupiter/Sun Trine, which is very rare. It means he has a unique and special personality. It's a combination of being very genuine, romantic, easygoing and very successful without having to be a "cutthroat" type. The two best careers for him would either be as an artist or in TV as an announcer. His chart is extremely positive. The only conflict is an internal struggle between a belief of science vs. religion. John is capable of producing such works as *X-Men/Alpha Flight*, *Union Jack* and the critical-ly acclaimed Western DESPERADOES.

LAURA DEPUY, in addition to being an award-winning colorist, is also a Nouveau Barrista. Among other coffee delights, Laura has designed *Café Sushá*, for Californians who want their sushi on the go. Laura divides her time between coloring PLANETARY, JLA, *Universe X* and *Ministry of Space* and her fiancé Randy.

DAVID BARON said he would like to do one of two things when he grew up: be a pro wrestler or make comic books. He decided upon comics. For now, anyway. Career highlights include working on PLANETARY and THE AUTHORITY. Future career highlights will include headlining stints on *NWF Smackdown*.